■SCHOLAST

Geronimo Stilton
ACADEMY

Vocabulary
Pawbook

2

Text by Geronimo Stilton
Based on the original idea by Elisabetta Dami
Illustrations by Piemme Archives

www.geronimostilton.com

© Atlantyca S.p.A. – via Leopardi 8, 20123 Milano, Italia – foreignrights@atlantyca.it

© 2015 for this Work in English language, Scholastic Education International (Singapore) Private Limited. A division of Scholastic Inc.
SCHOLASTIC and associated logos are trademarks and/or registered trademarks of Scholastic Inc.

Visit our website: www.scholastic.com.sg

First edition 2015

ISBN 978-981-4629-67-6

Welcome to the
Geronimo Stilton
ACADEMY

Well-loved for its humor, fascinating visuals and fun characters, the best-selling *Geronimo Stilton* series is enjoyed by children in many countries.

Research shows that learners learn better when they are engaged and motivated. The **Geronimo Stilton Academy: Vocabulary Pawbook** series builds on children's interest in Geronimo Stilton. It makes learning more accessible, and increases learners' motivation to read and expand their vocabulary.

The Geronimo Stilton Academy: Vocabulary Pawbook series comprises three levels:

Pawbook 1 (Junior level)	Pawbook 2 (Senior level)	Pawbook 3 (Master level)

• Word formations
• Word and sentence level activities
• Includes
  - theme-related nouns
  - verbs
  - suffixes
  - adjectives
  - synonyms
	• Word formations
	• Sentence and short text level activities
	• Includes
	  - prefixes
	  - synonyms / antonyms
	  - word clines
	  - idioms
	  - onomatopoeia
		• Word formations
		• Sentence and text level activities
		• Includes
		  - theme-related words and phrases
		  - synonyms / antonyms
		  - prefixes and suffixes
		  - word clines
		  - word analogies

Please refer to the contents page for a full list of topics.

Geronimo Stilton titles featured in this Pawbook:

© 2015 Scholastic Education International (S) Pte Ltd   ISBN 978-981-4629-67-6

Motivating learners
Authentic excerpts from *Geronimo Stilton* titles interest and encourage learners to read the rest of the story.

Expanding vocabulary
The 3-step format in each unit provides learners with examples of the words used in context, and helps expand vocabulary and understand their usage.

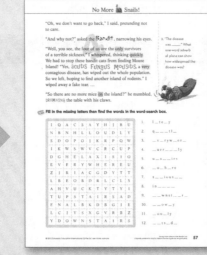

1 **Notes and examples** show new vocabulary in context, and **side-bar questions** stimulate learners to decipher meaning from contextual clues.

2 **Fun activities** introduce learners to the focus words in an accessible format.

3 **Sentence and text level activities** help assess learners' understanding of the new vocabulary and their ability to use it.

Consolidating learning
Each double-page spread consists of a fun activity related to the preceding units to help consolidate what students have learned.

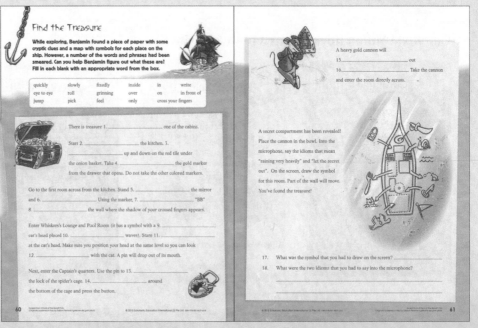

© 2015 Scholastic Education International (S) Pte Ltd   ISBN 978-981-4629-67-6

Contents

© 2015 Scholastic Education International (S) Pte Ltd ISBN 978-981-4629-67-6

1 I'm Afraid of Bugs!

My family thought that I was too scared of everything so they tricked me into enroling in a boot camp.

The jeep made its way along a paved road. Soon the road turned into a beaten track. Then it became a **MUDDY** path.

 It was so hot I felt like a walking sprinkler. I was dripping sweat! Clouds of mosquitoes swarmed around me. They were having a party in my fur. I figured my tail was their dinner. They were making a meal out of it. What if they gave me some rare disease?

  I'M AFRAID OF DISEASES!

We reached the camp in the middle of the night. It looked like an army barracks. It stood in the middle of a clearing surrounded by very tall trees.

I was so tired. I feel onto a smelly bunk bed. I tried not to think about the fleas that were probably crawling in it. Ugh!

 I'M AFRAID OF BUGS!

Exhausted, I fell asleep fully dressed. That night, I kept hearing Trap's voice in my dreams. "Just don't think about it!" he chanted over and over.

Descriptive words help to paint a picture of the setting that the events are taking place in. Here, they are used to give us Geronimo's first impression of the base camp and and how he felt when he got there.

 Chew on it!

1. From Geronimo's description, what kind of an image do you get of the camp? How does it make you feel?

Excerpt from *Four Mice Deep In The Jungle*
(Originally published in Italy by Edizioni Piemme *Quattro Topi Nella Giungla Nera*)   © 2015 Scholastic Education International (S) Pte Ltd   ISBN 978-981-4629-67-6

I'm Afraid of Bugs!

At dawn, Penelope gave me a wake-up call. She poured a bucketful of icy water on my head! "LINE UP!" she shrieked.

I looked outside. That's when I discovered there were four other mice taking this crazy jungle course.

2. Why do you think Geronimo uses the word "crazy" to describe the boot camp?

A. Unscramble the letters of the following words. The capital letters start the word.

1. h s d e a t x u **E** _____

2. e a i **O** r n n v h g g _____

3. n e g o n **U** d r r u d _____

4. c i n a **P**-t i k n s r c e _____

5. l n **J** e g u _____

6. a e y f **L** _____

7. d i r e f **T** r i e _____

8. m o s e **V** o n u _____

9. l d **M** y o _____

10. t g i n o **R** t _____

B. Complete the crossword puzzle with a suitable describing word. The first letter of each word is given to help you.

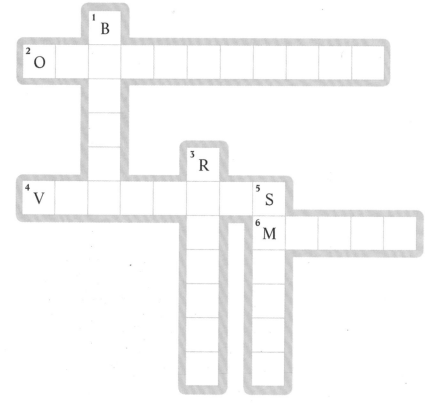

Across

2. The o_____ vines made the tree look like a monster in the dark.

4. Geronimo screamed when he saw the v_____ snake.

6. Geronimo was so hungry he would have eaten the m_____ mushrooms.

Down

1. Thea and Benjamin walked along the b_____ track until they came to the cottage.

3. The r_____ wood gave way under Geronimo's weight.

5. The bed was s_____ but Geronimo didn't care.

Excerpt from *Four Mice Deep In The Jungle*
(Originally published in Italy by Edizioni Piemme Quattro Topi Nella Giungla Nera)

I'm Afraid of Bugs!

A. Complete the sentences by matching the noun to the correct describing word.

1. After hiking for a whole day, Geronimo was   •

    _____.

2. The _____ trees provided shade.   •

3. This _____ species of spider can   •

    only be found here.

4. Geronimo stepped on the _____   •

    patch of grass and slipped.

5. As Geronimo looked over the edge of the cliff,   •

    he was _____.

• rare

• leafy

• terrified

• muddy

• exhausted

B. Replace the underlined describing word with one of your own so that the sentence still makes sense.

1. Geronimo bit into the <u>moldy</u> bread. _____

2. It was much easier to walk along the <u>paved</u> road than the

    muddy path. _____

3. When the fire went out, a <u>panic-stricken</u> Geronimo sat in

    the dark. _____

4. Penelope shot Geronimo a <u>venomous</u> stare that made his

    whiskers curl. _____

5. The tree's <u>underground</u> roots caused Geronimo to stumble. _____

Excerpt from *Four Mice Deep In The Jungle*
(Originally published in Italy by Edizioni Piemme Quattro Topi Nella Giungla Nera)

 ISBN 978-981-4629-67-6

Complete each sentence using the descriptive words indicated.

1. To help Geronomo overcome his fear of everything, Thea, Trap and Benjamin

   _____ (crazy).

2. When Geronimo was told he had to attend the survival camp,

   _____ (terrified).

3. Penelope was clearly crazy! Her idea of _____

   _____ (wake-up).

4. Instead of _____ (paved),

   Penelope made the recruits run on the muddy track.

5. It was so hot that Geronimo longed to _____

   _____ (leafy).

6. The trees with their _____

   _____ (overhanging).

Excerpt from *Four Mice Deep In The Jungle*
(Originally published in Italy by Edizioni Piemme Quattro Topi Nella Giungla Nera)

I made some new friends and we all survived the first day. Would we survive the second?

After lunch, it was back to marching. At last, we reached the Rio Mosquito.

A rope hung over the water, stretched between two trees. The river roared downstream, picking up anything in its path. I saw twigs. I saw tree trunks. I saw a houseboat filled with monkeys. Everything was swept away in the raging current.

"I'm scared!" I squeaked.

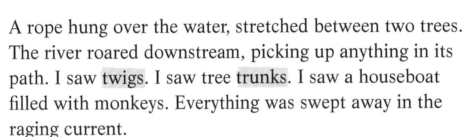

"I'M AFRAID OF DROWNING!"

Penelope rolled her eyes. "Get moving or you'll be sorry!" she demanded.

We did as we were told. What choice did we have? I grabbed the rope and began to cross the river. *One paw at a time*, I told myself. Slowly we made our way to the other side. I was doing it!

But suddenly, disaster struck. Someone was crying. "I'm so hungry! I'm going to faint!" Tubby wailed. Seconds later, the rope slipped from his paws. He hit the water with a loud splash. What could I do? I dove in after him.

A **word cline** is a list of words with similar meanings that vary in strength e.g. "squeak" is not as strong as "tell", and "tell" is not as strong as "demand".

Chew on it!

1. If "grabbed" is at one end of a word cline, what do you think would be at the other?

Excerpt from *Four Mice Deep In The Jungle*
(Originally published in Italy by Edizioni Piemme Quattro Topi Nella Giungla Nera)

© 2015 Scholastic Education International (S) Pte Ltd   ISBN 978-981-4629-67-6

Tubby's snout was already underwater. I quickly grabbed hold of his tail. Groaning, I dragged him onto the bank. Then I gave him mouse-to-mouse resuscitation. It worked!

"Thank you! You saved my life!" squeaked a grateful Tubby.

I grinned. I felt like Supermouse when he does a good deed. Too bad I wasn't really Supermouse. If I were, I could have flown right home! *Still, I was proud of myself for facing another fear.*

I guess Penelope was proud of me, too. "You're learning, Stilton!" she sniggered. "You're learning!"

2. Can you think of three other words that would be on the same word cline as "good"?

Fill in the missing letters of the words in the word clines.

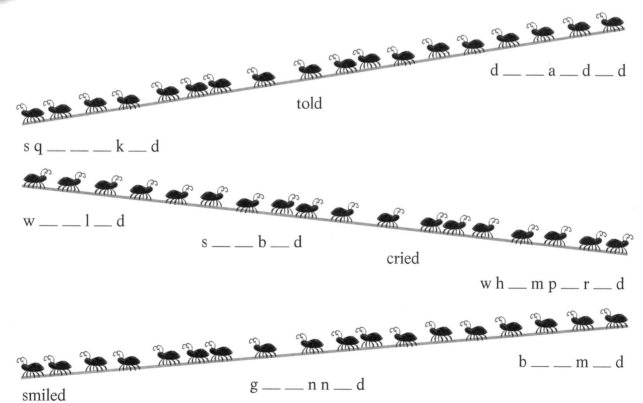

d __ __ a __ d __ d

told

s q __ __ __ k __ d

w __ __ l __ d

s __ __ b __ d

cried

w h __ m p __ r __ d

smiled

g __ __ n n __ d

b __ __ m __ d

Excerpt from *Four Mice Deep In The Jungle*
(Originally published in Italy by Edizioni Piemme Quattro Topi Nella Giungla Nera)

Fill in the blanks with the correct word from the word cline given.

> Word cline: smiled, grinned, beamed

1. After being saved, Tubby _____ weakly at
    Geronimo, who _____ back at him. Suzie
    Squeakers stood near by and _____ brightly at
    the two of them.

2. Tubby _____ from ear to ear as Suzie handed him some cheese
    sandwiches. She _____ shyly at him.

3. Benjamin was so proud that his uncle Geronimo had saved Tubby that he
    _____ like the sun.

> Word cline: twigs, branches, trunk

4. Geronimo scaled the _____ of the tree and sat on one of the
    _____. He then reached out and snapped two _____.

5. As Suzie gathered the _____ on the ground to
    get a fire going, a bird sat on one of the _____
    of the tree, watching her.

6. After hiking for half an hour, Tubby sat on the fallen
    _____ of a fallen tree to catch his breath.

> Word cline: hungry, famished, peckish, starving

7. Tubby said that he was _____ and he would practically eat a horse.

8. Even Geronimo agreed that he was _____ and the sandwiches they
    had were not enough. He knew he was _____ as his stomach was
    growling.

9. Suzie never ate much to begin with but after the dissatisfying meal, she too was
    feeling _____.

12 Excerpt from *Four Mice Deep In The Jungle*
(Originally published in Italy by Edizioni Piemme Quattro Topi Nella Giungla Nera)

© 2015 Scholastic Education International (S) Pte Ltd ISBN 978-981-4629-67-6

In the first column, fill in the word that corresponds to the meaning in the middle column. In the last column, write 1, 2, 3, or 4 to indicate the intensity of the word. (1 is the least and 4 is the most.)

1. Word cline: cry, sob, wail, whimper

Word	Meaning	Intensity
	to cry noisily with short gasps	
	to shed tears, either from sorrow, distress or pain	
	to make a loud, long cry of sadness or pain	
	to make a quiet crying sound	

2. Word cline: misfortune, mishap, disaster

Word	Meaning	Intensity
	an unlucky accident	
	an event that happens suddenly and causes great suffering and loss to many people	
	an unfortunate event	

3. Word cline: demand, tell, squeak

Word	Meaning	Intensity
	to say something to someone in a normal tone of voice	
	To say something to someone in an authoritative manner	
	to say something to someone in a high-pitched voice, usually from nervousness	

Excerpt from Four Mice Deep In The Jungle (Originally published in Italy by Edizioni Piemme Quattro Topi Nella Giungla Nera)

For three days, my fellow trainees and I braved the wilds of the jungle together so I wasn't prepared for what happened on Day 4…

The next morning, I woke up to a pair of singing birds. The sun warmed my fur. I stretched. For the first time since I'd arrived in the jungle, I felt great. But what was different about today? I just couldn't put my paw on it. Then it hit me — a bucketful of icy water right in my snout!

Penelope Poisonfur snickered, then she barked out orders. "LINE UP!" she squeaked. "Today you will learn to use a compass. Each of you must find your way to our next CAMPSITE before nightfall. And you must do it on your own!"

I shuddered. "BUT I'M AFRAID TO BE LEFT ON MY OWN IN THE FOREST!"

I cried. Too late. Everyone had already left. I was alone in the forest. This was worse than the time I got separated from my uncle Nbbles at the Marvelous Mouse Tail Circus. At least that time, the rat clowns kept me laughing. Now there wasn't a rodent in sight. Monkeys SHRIEKED at me from the trees. Snakes HISSED from behind rocks. Even the singing birds sounded SCARY. I jumped at every noise. I was like a furry rubber band ready to snap.

I decided I'd better study the map. *This will be as easy as cheesepie*, I told myself. All I had to do was figure out how to get to the camp. "Um, let's see," I mumbled. "I am here, or maybe I'm here. And then I'm headed there — or maybe there?" I checked the compass. North, South, East, West. It wasn't as easy as I'd thought. I tried giving myself a pep talk. … "Just use your brain!" But my brain must have been taking

A **hyponym** is a more specific term for something that belongs to a larger group of similar items. For example, "fur", "paw" and "snout" are all hyponyms for animal body parts.

Chew on it!

1. What are some hyponyms that would be part of the group "forest"?

a cheese break. Half an hour later, I burst into tears. "Rotten rat's teeth!" I squeaked. *"I'm lost!"*

2. If "teeth" is a hyponym of the lower part of a face, what other hyponyms can you think of that would be in the same category?

A. Fill in the missing letters of the hyponyms for animals.

		S		A		E	S	
	R		E	N		S		
				I		D	S	
				M		N	E	S
			R	A		S		
C			C	D		L	S	
		T		G		S		

B. Label the animal body parts. Use the list to help you.

snout
fur
paw
tail
whiskers

C. Do you know your compass directions? Fill in the blanks with the correct hyponym.

N_____

N_____w_____   N_____e_____

W_____   E_____

S_____w_____   S_____e_____

S_____

A. Here are a list of hyponyms of the body parts of different animals. Do you know which animals they belong to? Fill in each blank with the correct animal, either mouse, fish, bird or deer.

1. beak _____
2. paw _____
3. gill _____
4. snout _____
5. feather _____

6. scale _____
7. hoof _____
8. wing _____
9. fin _____
10. antler _____

B. The various nouns are missing in the following passage. Fill in each blank with an appropriate word from the box. You may not need to use all of them.

rodent	shrieked	paw	rocks	water	forests
hissed	monkeys	snakes	squeaked	birds	trees

We entered the forest. 1. _____ as tall as skyscrapers surrounded us.

The foliage was so thick we couldn't see any sunlight. The 2. _____

was home to all kinds of animals. They called to one another as we passed by.

3. _____, 4. _____, and

5. _____ watched our every move. We were like

6. _____ celebrities at an awards show.

 Excerpt from Four Mice Deep In The Jungle (Originally published in Italy by Edizioni Piemme Quattro Topi Nella Giungla Nera) © 2015 Scholastic Education International (S) Pte Ltd ISBN 978-981-4629-67-6

Where are they standing? Fill in the blanks with the correct compass directions. (The compass in the middle denotes base camp.)

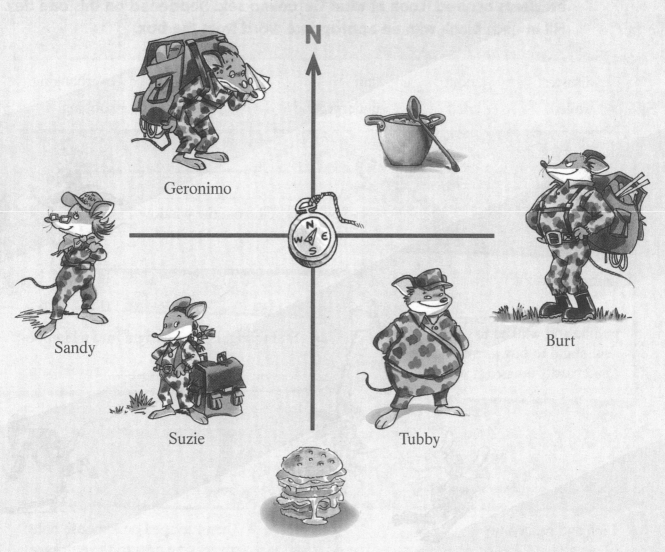

1. Burt is to the _____ of base camp while Sandy is to the

   _____.

2. If you walk _____ from base camp, you will find Suzie.

3. Geronimo is hungry. He would have to walk _____ to get to

   the base camp, and then walk _____ to get to the burger.

4. Tubby is hungry too and wants some soup. To get it, he will have

   to walk _____ to base camp before walking

   _____ to get to the soup.

© 2015 Scholastic Education International (S) Pte Ltd ISBN 978-981-4629-67-6

Excerpt from *Four Mice Deep In The Jungle*
(Originally published in Italy by Edizioni Piemme Quattro Topi Nella Giungla Nera)

THE TRANSFORMATION

A. Geronimo was afraid of everything. Each time he left his mouse hole, accidents occured. Look at what Geronimo said happened on this one day. Fill in each blank with an appropriate word from the box.

disaster	snout	tail	muddy	overhanging
wailed	cried	underground	paved	sobbing

1 I jumped over a _____ puddle and walked to the newsstand to buy a paper. I had hardly opened it when …

2 A _____ flowerpot fell from the window ledge, hitting me on the head.

3 Stumbling, I crashed right into a lamppost. I _____ out in pain.

4 Then I tripped on a mouse hole cover lying next to the entrance to the _____ sewers.

5 I fell and bashed my _____ on the hard _____ walkway.

6 As I sat there _____, a taxi ran over my _____.

7 I _____ loudly. Then a pigeon decided to poop on my nose. What a _____!

Excerpt from *Four Mice Deep In The Jungle* (Originally published in Italy by Edizioni Piemme Quattro Topi Nella Giungla Nera)

© 2015 Scholastic Education International (S) Pte Ltd ISBN 978-981-4629-67-6

B. After Geronimo attended the boot camp, he returned to Dr. Shrinkfur, the psychiatrist that Thea had recommended. Fill in each blank with an appropriate word from the box and read what he told the doctor.

At first I thought I would go 1. _____. When I first went to the

2. _____ camp, I was 3. _____ of the dark.

But after spending a few nights in the 4. _____, I no longer fear it.

I encountered 5. _____ snakes, 6. _____ and

7. _____, snapping 8. _____, and mischievous

9. _____, but I'm no longer scared of these animals.

I learned how to read the directions on a compass — 10. _____,

11. _____, 12. _____,

13. _____. And when the compass didn't help, I climbed a

14. _____ tree, sat on its 15. _____ branches,

and conquered my fear of heights. Doctor, I'm cured!

spiders	scorpions	crazy	jungle	monkeys
North	very tall	West	venomous	East
crocodiles	army	South	terrified	overhanging

Excerpt from Four Mice Deep In The Jungle (Originally published in Italy by Edizioni Piemme Quattro Topi Nella Giungla Nera)

An elderly female rodent had accused me of being rude to her. But I had never seen her before. It was a horrible start to my morning. What more could happen?

I headed toward the **SUBWAY**. At the station, I ran into a friend of mine. His name is Benny Bluewhiskers, but most rodents call him the Big Cheese. That's because he knows everything there is to know about CHEESES — COLOR, size, shape, texture. He even invented Mouse Island's famous cheese measurer. …

As soon as he saw me, Benny frowned. … "I know I'm not the thinnest rodent in town, but you didn't have to call me a furry whale with a tail!" Benny shrieked. … "I thought we were friends."

I looked at him in shock. Cheese niblets! "But I wasn't at *The Nibbler* last night," I tried to explain.

That seemed to make Benny even madder. "So now you're calling me a liar!" he squeaked. "Well, that's it! No more free cheese for you! And you can forget my holiday cheddar log this year, too!"

I didn't know what to say. My head was spinning faster than the cyclone at the Mouseyland Amusement Park.

Un-be-liev-a-ble!

I stumbled into my office, still in a daze. … Right then, the phone rang. "Hello? Stilton speaking, *Geronimo Stilton*!" I answered.

We use **comparative adjectives** to compare two things. We form the comparative by adding
- "-er" / "-ier"
- "more" to some words

We use superlative adjectives to compare three or more things. We form the superlative by adding
- "-ier" / "iest"
- "most" to some words

Some words like "good" change their form completely.

 Chew on it!

1. Rephrase Benny's statement "I thought we were friends" using a comparative. (Hint: What if Benny had said, "I thought we were good friends."?)

 Excerpt from *Paws Off, Cheddarface!* (Originally published in Italy by Edizioni Piemme *Giù le zampe, faccia di fontina!*) © 2015 Scholastic Education International (S) Pte Ltd ISBN 978-981-4629-67-6

It was Simon Squealer. He was the most famous radio host in New Mouse City. His show was all gossip. …

"Today we are speaking to Geronimo Stilton, best-selling author and publisher of popular newspaper *The Rodent's Gazette*," the host began babbling. "Yes, you're on the air, Stilton!" he finished.

2. Can you identify two words in the superlative form in the passage?

Draw a continuous line by finding the comparative forms of the listed words. Start from the colored square and go in the direction of the arrow. The line should stop at the square marked "END".

bad	fast	juicy	scary	badly
funny	mad	silly	big	furry
neat	talented	boring	good	popular
unbelievable	famous	handsome	scared	wacky

P	U	M	O	F	U	R	R	I	E	R	M	O
O	L	A	U	R	D	E	R	A	C	S	E	R
P	A	F	S	E	W	O	R	S	E	N	E	A
E	R	E	B	I	T	E	R	O	M	R	E	T
R	M	R	I	L	A	L	E	N	T	E	D	END
O	A	O	G	L	L	B	A	V	E	I	J	R
M	D	M	G	I	E	↓	N	B	E	L	U	E
R	D	R	E	S	M	M	U	E	R	O	I	I
E	E	E	R	R	O	O	T	E	R	M	C	K
T	R	I	F	E	R	R	S	A	F	Y	I	C
T	S	R	U	I	E	E	B	A	D	L	E	A
E	C	A	N	N	B	H	E	R	O	M	R	W
B	G	N	I	R	O	A	N	D	S	O	M	E

A. **A superlative is the form of an adjective that denotes that something is of the highest quality in that area. Circle the correct superlative in the following sentences.**

1. Benny Bluewhiskers was the most famous / famousest sniffer in New Mouse City.

2. Trap was the baddest / worst prankster in the family.

3. Simon Squealer thought that Geronimo had the juiciest / most juicy gossip for his listeners.

4. Geronimo's feelings were badlyiest / most badly hurt when Benny refused to give him any more free cheese.

5. Benjamin was the best / goodest nephew that Geronimo had.

B. **Fill in each blank with either the comparative or superlative form of the adjective in the brackets.**

1. Benny Bluewhiskers was _____ (mad) than the elderly female rodent was at Geronimo.

2. This was the _____ (boring) article on the front page.

3. Being the _____ (scared) in the group, Geronimo stayed at the back when they entered the room.

4. That was the _____ (silly) joke that Trap had ever played on Geronimo.

5. Talking to Simon Squealer was _____ (scary) than being scolded by the elderly female mouse.

6. Thea was _____ (talented) in cooking pasta than Trap was in making pizzas.

Excerpt from *Paws Off, Cheddarface!*
(Originally published in Italy by Edizioni Piemme *Giù le zampe, faccia di fontina!*)

© 2015 Scholastic Education International (S) Pte Ltd ISBN 978-981-4629-67-6

Rewrite each sentence, first with a comparative then with a superlative form of the adjective in bold, and using the words in the brackets. An example has been done for you.

Example:

	Geronimo is **neat**.
comparative (Thea):	Geronimo is neater than Thea.
superlative (in the office):	Geronimo is the neatest in the office.

1.   *The Rodent's Gazette* is a **popular** newspaper.
     comparative (*The Daily Rat*):

     _____

     superlative (in New Mouse City):

     _____

2.   Thea told a **wacky** story.
     comparative (Trap):

     _____

     superlative (of them all):

     _____

3.   Trap is **funny**.
     comparative (Geronimo):

     _____

     superlative (in the family):

     _____

4.   Benjamin is a **fast** runner.
     comparative (Thea):

     _____

     superlative (in his class):

     _____

5.   Geronimo's story is **unbelievable**.
     comparative (Benjamin):

     _____

     superlative (of all stories):

     _____

Excerpt from *Paws Off, Cheddarface!*

My day was getting worse. So many people were accusing me of doing things I hadn't done! What would happen next?

A crowd of rodents was waiting in front of my mouse hole. "**There he is!** That's him!" I heard them shout.

Oh, no. They must have seen the posters of me and the Flusher Rat. Maybe they wanted to ask me about toilet paper.

A reporter stuck a microphone under my snout. "Mr. Stilton, I am Colin Chattermouse from . Do you really believe that watching TV is better than reading a book?" he asked.

"Cheese niblets!" I squeaked. "That's ridiculous! Why would I, *Geronimo Stilton*, say such a thing? I am the publisher of *The Rodent's Gazette*, the most popular paper in New Mouse City. I am a best-selling author. Only an IGNORANT, ILLITERATE, INCOMPETENT, UNEDUCATED, THICK-HEADED FURBRAIN would say something so foolish!"

But before I could go on, the reporter waved a newspaper under my snout. "Then how do you explain this?" he challenged. I gasped. The front page showed a picture of me holding a remote control in one paw. In the other paw, I held up a garbage can. It was filled with books! STILTON SAYS, "BOOKS ARE FOR BABIES, TELEVISION IS OUR FRIEND!" the headline read.

Just then, the phone rang. I picked it up. I shouldn't have. The rodent on the other end gave me some horrible news. I was being kicked out of the *Press Club*. "No respectable newspapermouse would throw away books!" he snorted.

Geronimo uses a range of synonyms to describe someone who lacks knowledge. Most words can usually be replaced by another, although their meaning may not be exactly the same. One example is "snorted" (meaning "made a disapproving sound") and "grunted" (meaning "made a short, low sound"). Though their meanings are different, they are considered synonyms as both relate to making a sound to show an emotion or opinion.

 Chew on it!

1. What one word synonym would you use to replace "go on"?

2. In what other way could you say "I picked it up"?

Excerpt from *Paws Off, Cheddarface!*
(Originally published in Italy by Edizioni Piemme *Giù le zampe, faccia di fontina!*)

© 2015 Scholastic Education International (S) Pte Ltd ISBN 978-981-4629-67-6

A Thick-headed Furbrain

What are these words? Using the key on the right, replace the numbers with their corresponding letters. Once you have the words, answer the question.

A	1
B	2
C	3
D	4
E	5
F	6
G	7
H	8
I	9
J	10
K	11
L	12
M	13
N	14
O	15
P	16
Q	17
R	18
S	19
T	20
U	21
V	22
W	23
X	24
Y	25
Z	26

1. 2 18 15 1 4 19 8 5 5 20

2. 18 5 6 21 19 5   2 9 14

3. 9 14 3 15 13 16 5 20 5 14 20

4. 20 18 21 19 20 23 15 18 20 8 25

5. 20 1 2 12 15 9 4

6. 5 24 3 12 1 9 13 5 4

7. 19 14 15 18 20 5 4

8. 20 18 1 19 8   3 1 14

9. 7 18 21 14 20 5 4

10. 18 5 19 16 5 3 20 1 2 12 5

11. 21 14 5 4 21 3 1 20 5 4

12. 7 1 19 16 5 4

Which two words are synonyms for "honorable"?

_____ and _____.

Excerpt from *Paws Off, Cheddarface!*
(Originally published in Italy by Edizioni Piemme *Giù le zampe, faccia di fontina!*)

Synonyms do not always have exactly the same meaning. Look at the following groups of words. For each group, match the words in the boxes with the meanings given.

| newspaper | broadsheet | tabloid | paper |

1. _____ a regular printed publication made up of folded unstapled sheets that normally contain news, articles and advertisements

2. _____ a regular printed publication that normally deals with serious subjects

3. _____ the shortened form of "newspaper"

4. _____ a regular printed publication that usually has sensational stories

| reputable | trustworthy | respectable | honorable |

5. _____ having a dependable nature

6. _____ having a good reputation

7. _____ having honesty and good moral character

8. _____ having a decent character, appearance or behavior

| illiterate | uneducated | incompetent | ignorant |

9. _____ lacking the necessary skills or ability to do something

10. _____ lacking a high level of education

11. _____ lacking information or knowledge

12. _____ lacking the ability to read or write

Excerpt from *Paws Off, Cheddarface!*
(Originally published in Italy by Edizioni Piemme *Giù le zampe, faccia di fontina!*)

© 2015 Scholastic Education International (S) Pte Ltd ISBN 978-981-4629-67-6

A Thick-headed  Furbrain

 A. **Antonyms are words that have the opposite meaning of another e.g. the antonym of the word "synonym" is "antonym". Fill the following blanks with the appropriate antonym from the box.**

literate	educated	intelligent	indecent

1. respectable _____

2. thick-headed _____

3. illiterate _____

4. uneducated _____

B. **Complete the passage with antonyms of the words in the brackets.**

Geronimo was having a bad day. When he awoke this morning, he was a respectable

newspapermouse. Now they were calling him 1. _____ (trustworthy),

2. _____ (honorable), and accusing him

of so many things he would never even dream of doing.

He was becoming 3. _____ (reputable)!

He was a 4. _____ (incompetent)

and 5. _____ (ignorant) mouse.

Something was suspicious. He had to find out what was going on.

C. **Which word from the passage do you think is the antonym of the following words?**

1. treasure chest _____

2. unknown _____

3. accepted _____

4. fantastic _____

Excerpt from *Paws Off, Cheddarface!*
(Originally published in Italy by Edizioni Piemme *Giù le zampe, faccia di fontina!*)

Stilton, Old Pal...

> I thought I could escape to the safety of my mouse hole. How wrong I was!

I was miserable. Then I noticed the light blinking on my answering machine. I raced over to it. Maybe I had some **happy messages**. Maybe my favorite nephew had called. …

The first message was from some rodent named Stuart Swingtail. He said he was a **singer** at the **SLEAZY FUR DANCE FACTORY!** I frowned. I'd never been there. Only sewer rats hung out at the Sleazy Fur. So what was this Swingtail mouse calling *me* for?

"Hey Stilton, old pal! You were really kicking up those paws Saturday night!" he squeaked. "By the way, you owe me fifty smackers. Don't forget, pal. See you next week at the factory!"

DR. EDWARD S. SMUGRAT III

The second message was from Dr. Edward S. Smugrat III. He was a very rich and STUCK-UP mouse. He had the best golf clubs, the best golf shoes, and the best golf shirts. Still he was an awful golfer. I guess it's true what they say, clothes do not make a mouse.

"Stilton! What do you think you are twying to pull?" Smugrat shrieked. "I know you swiped my Wat King cwedit card! I just got the bill for your dinner with fifty-seven fwiends at the **golf club**. You will be heawing fwom my lawyer!"

Figurative expressions are colorful ways of saying something and do not give the literal meaning of words. They include metaphors, idioms and hyperboles. For example, "sewer rats" is a term used to describe people who are dirty, useless and disgusting. It comes from the idea that rats in the sewer are dirty and usually create problems for human beings.

 Chew on it!

1. What do you think is the original phrase of "clothes do not make a mouse"?

Excerpt from *Paws Off, Cheddarface!*
(Originally published in Italy by Edizioni Piemme *Giù le zampe, faccia di fontina!*)

After that came a message from a Mr. Van Der Raten. He owned an antiques shop called Treasured Crumbs. The antiques in his place were more expensive than my cousin Brainypaw's college tuition!

Still, Mr. Van Der Raten said that I had purchased a solid-gold cheese holder just yesterday. "I gave you the cheese holder on good faith," he said. "I know you are a respectable newspapermouse. But you will need to come in to settle your bill."

Mr. Van Der Raten

2. Do you think "Treasured Crumbs" is a figurative expression? Why?

 **Find the answers to the crossword using the figurative expressions given in the clues.**

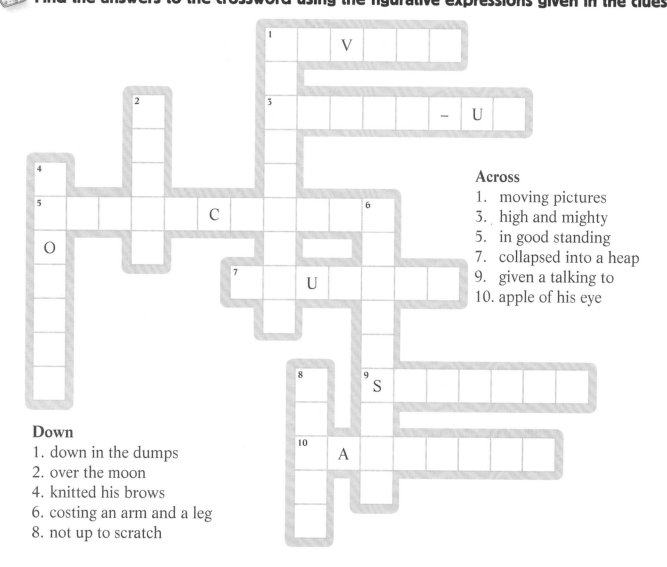

Across
1. moving pictures
3. high and mighty
5. in good standing
7. collapsed into a heap
9. given a talking to
10. apple of his eye

Down
1. down in the dumps
2. over the moon
4. knitted his brows
6. costing an arm and a leg
8. not up to scratch

© 2015 Scholastic Education International (S) Pte Ltd ISBN 978-981-4629-67-6

Excerpt from *Paws Off, Cheddarface!*
(Originally published in Italy by Edizioni Piemme *Giù le zampe, faccia di fontina!*)

A. **The following figurative expressions appear in the passage. Do you know what they mean?**

1. kicking up those paws (heels)

   _____

2. fifty smackers

   _____

3. clothes do not make the mouse (man)

   _____

4. on good faith

   _____

5. settle your bill

   _____

B. **Fill in each blank with a figurative expression given in the clues for the crossword puzzle. Make sure that the sentences read correctly.**

1. The first message was from Stuart Swingtail, a singer at the
   SLEAZY FUR DANCE FACTORY.

   I _____ .Why would he be calling me?

2. Being wrongly accused of things he did not do made

   Geronimo feel _____ .

   He _____ on the floor and moped.

3. All the antiques in Mr. Van Der Raten's shop _____ .
   Gerinomo could never be able to afford anything.

4. Geronimo was _____ to hear Benjamin's voice on the

   phone. His nephew was _____ .

5. Dr. Edward S. Smugrat III acted _____

   but his golf game was _____ .

 Excerpt from *Paws Off, Cheddarface!*
(Originally published in Italy by Edizioni Piemme *Giù le zampe, faccia di fontina!*)   © 2015 Scholastic Education International (S) Pte Ltd ISBN 978-981-4629-67-6

A. Some words can be substituted with figurative expressions. Which words do the following refer to?

1   in high spirits   _____

2.   close to one's heart   _____

3.   out of sorts   _____

4.   furrowed one's brows   _____

5.   of good repute   _____

B. Create sentences with the following figurative expressions.

1.   moving pictures

_____

_____

2.   settle the bill

_____

_____

3.   out of sorts

_____

_____

4.   kicking up one's heels

_____

_____

5.   over the moon

_____

_____

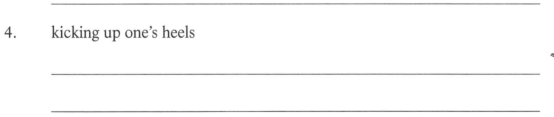

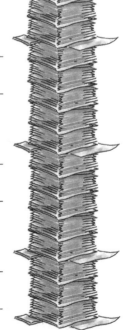

Excerpt from *Paws Off, Cheddarface!*
(Originally published in Italy by Edizioni Piemme *Giù le zampe, faccia di fontina!*)

THE IMPOSTER'S ANTICS

Someone who looked exactly like Geronimo was performing at the Pawprint Theater. Geronimo sat in the audience and watched. He couldn't believe what he saw.

Geronimo Stilton

LIVE ONSTAGE!

LIVE ONSTAGE!

at the
Pawprint Theater
7:30 p.m.

Don't miss Geronimo Stilton in this musical extravaganza!
Dancing, Squeaking, Cat Jokes, and more.
It's fun for the whole furry family!

LIVE ONSTAGE! LIVE ONSTAGE! LIVE ONSTAGE!

The imposter threw his hat into the crowd and started to tap-dance. It was _____1_____. He looked exactly like me!

Geronimo's double wore a _____2_____ little skirt made of bananas and a pineapple hat. He started singing and shaking a pair of maracas. He then did different dance routines.

The lookalike changed into a Spanish outfit and held a rose between his teeth. He looked like he was _____3_____.

Excerpt from *Paws Off, Cheddarface!*
(Originally published in Italy by Edizioni Piemme *Giù le zampe, faccia di fontina!*)

He came onstage in a tuxedo and sang the aria from an opera. He acted like the _____4_____ tenor in the world but it was off-key.

His costume got _____5_____. He came out in oversized clothes and started to rap.

Dressed as a serious actor, he started to recite from Shakespeare … badly. Obviously he was _____6_____.

Dressed as a clown, he had a red cherry taped to his nose. A huge piece of cheese sat on his head. He told a few jokes. This was the _____7_____ costume of them all.

Fill in the blanks in the boxes with one of the following words or phrases. Write the number in the space provided below.

wackiest   _____   unbelievable   _____

most talented   _____   wacky   _____

not up the scratch   _____   kicking up his paws   _____

wackier   _____

© 2015 Scholastic Education International (S) Pte Ltd ISBN 978-981-4629-67-6

Excerpt from *Paws Off, Cheddarface!*
(Originally published in Italy by Edizioni Piemme *Giù le zampe, faccia di fontina!*)

7 Garlic, Garlic, and More Garlic

A mysterious phone call from Trap had Thea, Benjamin and I on our way to Transratania, in search of Ratoff Castle…

We climbed off the train and looked around. Now we just had to figure out how to get to Ratoff Castle.

"Excuse me, sir, which way to Ratoff Castle?" I asked a tall, lean rat, wearing a ragged coat. His eyes opened wide. He clutched at his garlic necklace. Then he disappeared into the fog without a word.

My sister rolled her eyes. "Let me try," she grumbled. "You are absolutely useless, Germeister!" She tapped the arm of a passing female mouse. "Excuse me, could you direct me to Count Vlad von Ratoff's castle?" she said.

"**Aaaaiii!**" shrieked the mouse. She scampered off, shaking her bracelet of garlic cloves in the air.

We decided to check out the souvenir shop across from the station. A mouse with a crooked tail stood behind the counter. He looked at us with curiosity.

"Pardon me," I began.
"Ye-es?" said the mouse. …
"We're looking for the castle of
COUNT VON RATOFF," I finished.

At the name *Ratoff*, the mouse's eyes nearly popped out of his furry face. … Before I knew it, the mouse was shoving us out the door. He clicked the lock behind us and turned out the lights. …

Phrasal verbs are two-word phrases that consist of a verb and a particle, usually a preposition (e.g. clutched at) or an adverb (e.g. scampered off).

Chew on it!

1. What does "check out" mean?

2. Can you think of other phrasal verbs that contain the word "popped"? What does each one mean?

Excerpt from *Red Pizzas for a Blue Count*
(Originally published in Italy by Edizioni Piemme *Una granita di mosche per il Conte*)

© 2015 Scholastic Education International (S) Pte Ltd ISBN 978-981-4629-67-6

A few minutes later, we passed a fancy restaurant. I read the menu out loud. "Hearty garlic pot pie, jumbo garlic burgers, pasta with extra garlic . . ." What a strange menu! A large mouse came to the door. "Would you like to have dinner, sir?" he asked. His breath smelled like he had just sampled very dish on the menu.

"No, thank you," I gasped. "But could you tell us how to get to the castle of Count von Ratoff?"

In a flash, the mouse pulled out a big bottle and gulped down the liquid inside. Judging by the stench, it must have been garlic juice.

Complete the crossword with the verb in each phrasal verb. Can you tell where each word should be? The phrasal verbs have been grouped by the number of letters in the verb.

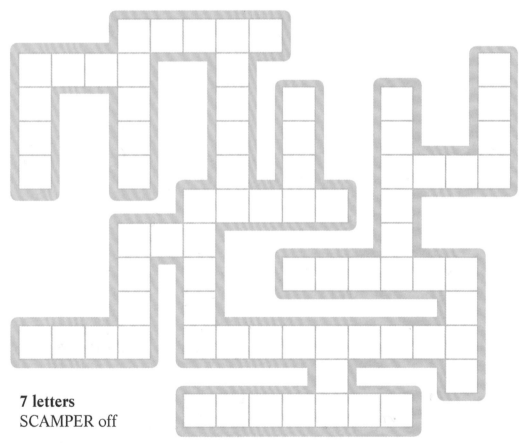

3 letters
GET to
POP out

4 letters
CAME to
GIVE way
GULP down
KEEP away
LOOK at
PASS by
PULL out
TURN out

5 letters
CHECK out
CLIMB down
SHAKE off
STAND up

6 letters
CLUTCH at
DIRECT to
FIGURE out

7 letters
SCAMPER off

9 letters
DISAPPEAR into

A. **Would you use a verb or a phrasal verb in each of the following sentences? Circle the right answer.**

1. Trap rolled up / rolled his sleeves and helped Thea move her couch.

2. They didn't see the mouse behind the counter until he stood / stood up.

3. Geronimo checked / checked out his luggage to make sure he had warm clothes.

4. The weather in Transratania was always foggy and cold. That was enough to keep / keep away all visitors.

5. Trap filled the balloon with so much air that it popped out / popped!

6. Benjamin climbed / climbed down the tree so he could see where everyone was from a higher position.

B. **Fill in each blank with either a phrasal verb or a verb in its correct form.**

1. Benjamin heard someone _____ (scamper) into the alley.

2. Geronimo _____ (gulp) when he heard that Trap was in Transratania.

3. The shopkeeper _____ (turn) the lights in the shop at the end of the day.

4. Geronimo tried to _____ (shake) the dust that clung to his coat.

5. Geronimo helped Benjamin _____ (pull) the splinter from his paw.

6. They followed the strange-looking mouse, but when they turned the corner, he had _____ (disappear)!

Excerpt from *Red Pizzas for a Blue Count*
(Originally published in Italy by Edizioni Piemme *Una granita di mosche per il Conte*)

© 2015 Scholastic Education International (S) Pte Ltd ISBN 978-981-4629-67-6

A verb can be combined with a number of particles to form phrasal verbs that have different meanings. Fill in each blank with the appropriate particle from the box.

by	down	around	away	out	up	off

When Geronimo heard that sweet Granny Onewhisker had passed 1. _____, he passed 2. _____. Trap couldn't pass 3. _____ the chance to make some money out of it and passed 4. _____ a hat at the office to gather donations. Thea heard a rumour when she passed 5. _____ the newsstand, that someone was claiming to be Granny's son to get the famous cheese souffle recipe that she had promised to pass 6. _____ to Geronimo. Thea was suspicious. Someone must be trying to pass himself 7. _____ as her son!

out	way	away	off	up	back

Benjamin has always been a sensitive, kind-hearted little mouse. He would always give 8. _____ to others and give 9. _____ his seat on the bus to someone who needs it more. Geronimo believes Benjamin might even give 10. _____ the shirt off his back! Today, as the little mouse helped out in the soup kitchen, giving 11. _____ hot bowls of stew, he encountered a strange mouse that gave 12. _____ the scent of rotting cheese. "Give me 13. _____ my book!" said the stranger.

out	down	up	after	for	through	into

Thea had been acting mysteriously so Geronimo felt he had to look 14. _____ the situation. After all, he was her big brother and had to look 15. _____ for her. If he didn't look 16. _____ his sister's welfare, who would? When she left her handbag in his office, he quickly looked 17. _____ it for clues. He was looking 18. _____ into the bag when Thea walked into his office looking 19. _____ it. "Ahem!" she said. Geronimo looked 20. _____ and gave her a sheepish smile.

 Excerpt from *Red Pizzas for a Blue Count*
(Originally published in Italy by Edizioni Piemme *Una granita di mosche per il Conte*)

We finally got to Ratoff Castle and managed to sneak inside. From our hiding place we saw the hunchback and two strange mice…

We followed the strange mice back into the castle. "Everyone keep their tails low and don't make a squeak," I instructed the others.

"Squeak!" whispered Thea, winking at me. *Why, oh, why will no one ever listen to me?* I thought in despair.

Hiding in the shadows, we crept quietly after the hunchback as he slunk toward the kitchen. A huge soup pot sat on the stove. He stuck a wooden spoon into the pot and tried to stir the contents. …

Eventually, the hunchback's spoon got stuck. "**CREEPYCRAWLYCRABAPPLES!**" shrieked the rodent. He began to pull on the spoon with all his might.

There was a *SUCKING* sound, and out flew the spoon. It hit the wall and stuck there. The hunchback stared at the spoon, then snickered. He bounced over to a huge GONG and hit it with a big hammer.

I peeked into the dining room. The count and the young countess were sitting at opposite ends of a very long table. The hunchback carried two crystal goblets over to the table. Then he poured a THICK RED liquid into each one. **I GULPED.** I had a feeling this was no cherry berry punch. It looked just like blood!

Onomatopoeia is the use of words that imitate the sounds things make. Some are very obvious like "meow" (the sound a cat makes) and "buzz" (the sound a bee makes). Others might not be so easy to discern such as "whisper" and "shiver".

 Chew on it!

1. Do you think "bounced" is an onomatopoeic word? Why?

Excerpt from *Red Pizzas for a Blue Count*
(Originally published in Italy by Edizioni Piemme *Una granita di mosche per il Conte*)

© 2015 Scholastic Education International (S) Pte Ltd   ISBN 978-981-4629-67-6

"How yummy!" said the young countess. She wiped her snout with a napkin, leaving DEEP RED SMUDGES.

I shivered. The sight of BLOOD makes me faint.

"Let's explore the castle while they are having their meal," I whispered. …

"Poor Uncle Trap! I wonder what's happened to him!" SOBBED Benjamin, blowing his nose. He really is such a sweet, sensitive mouse.

2. Can you think of some onomatopoeic words to make a story spooky?

Complete the word puzzle with the given onomatopoeic words. The words will only read downwards and the grid will not make sense when read across. One has been done for you. Then, complete the sentence below using the circled letters.

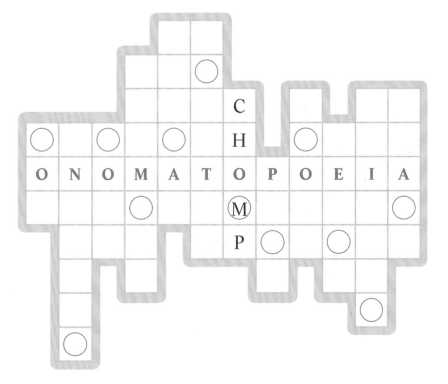

belch
chatter
chomp
clang
flicker
gong
grumble
knock
phew
snicker
sob
squeak

_E_O_I_O, T__A AND __NJAMI_ TO THE _E__UE!

Gonnnggg! Gonnnggg!

belch	chatter	chomp	clang	flicker
gong	grumble	gulp	knock	phew
shiver	shriek	slink	slurp	snicker
sob	squeak	whisper	whoosh	yummy

A.   Which onomatopoeic words would you use for the following? Choose words from the box above.

1.   to show the food is delicious   _____

2.   to show that someone is speaking softly,
     using his breath   _____

3.   to show a loud and rather prolonged metallic sound   _____

4.   to show someone crying noisily, to the point of
     gasping   _____

5.   to show someone is very relieved   _____

6.   to show someone chewing very loudly   _____

7.   to show that something is moving very quickly   _____

8.   to show a smooth, gliding movement   _____

9.   to show a high-pitched sound uttered in fear   _____

10. to show teeth clicking together repeatedly
     due to the cold   _____

B.   Replace the words in bold with an onomatopoeia. Use the same form of the word.

1.   Lightning flashed through the sky, causing the
     lights in Ratoff Castle to **blink rapidly on and off**.   _____

2.   Geronimo **complained unhappily** about being there.   _____

Excerpt from *Red Pizzas for a Blue Count*
(Originally published in Italy by Edizioni Piemme *Una granita di mosche per il Conte*)   © Scholastic Education International (S) Pte Ltd ISBN 978-981-4629-67-6

3. Benjamin hit the **large metallic disk** with the hammer. _____

4. Thea gave a **short, quiet and disrespectful laugh** at the thought of Geronimo feeling queasy about blood. _____

5. We **moved slowly and quietly so as not to be noticed** towards the door. _____

6. The hunchback **made a sucking sound when drinking** his soup. _____

For each pair of onomatopoeic words, create one sentence that contains both of them.

1. slink, whisper

_____

_____

2. chomp, grumble

_____

_____

3. slurp, yummy

_____

_____

4. clang, chatter

_____

_____

5. gulp, shriek

_____

_____

© 2015 Scholastic Education International (S) Pte Ltd ISBN 978-981-4629-67-6
Excerpt from *Red Pizzas for a Blue Count*
(Originally published in Italy by Edizioni Piemme *Una granita di mosche per il Conte*)

9 Please, Let Me Faint in Peace!

We found Trap. … And then we lost him again. Now we have to find him once more…

"I still don't understand how you convinced Count von Ratoff to let you stay," Thea remarked. "I mean, he doesn't exactly seem like Mr. Friendly Rat."

More like Mr. Frightening, I thought. But I didn't say a word. They would just call me a scaredy mouse.

"Old Ratoff doesn't know about my research," my cousin **chuckled**. "I just got myself hired as a cook. Which reminds me, tomorrow they'll be having a great ball here at the castle. I have to figure out the menu. The count and his niece have unusual tastes. They cannot stand garlic, but they love all kinds of insects! Strange huh? I don't ask. I just cook. Maybe I should make a nice BLOODSUCKER'S PIE, with my hearty BLOOD SAUSAGE filling," Trap said thoughtfully. "A creamy BLOOD PUDDING would make a tasty dessert. What do you think, Cousin?" …

Before Trap could continue, the bookcase he had been leaning against swiveled around and he disappeared!

"Trap!" we all shouted. But there was no answer. …

"We need to find out what happened to Trap," I said. "But how can we explore the castle without attracting attention?"

My nephew tugged at my sleeve. "I know! I know, Uncle!" he squeaked. "We'll pretend we are looking for jobs. They

A **prefix** is a group of letters added to the front of a word that changes its meaning. For example, the prefix "un-" means "not" so we can add "un-" to "usual" to get "unusual", which means "not usual".

Chew on it!

1. Add the prefixes "un-" and "re-" to "think". How do the prefixes change the meaning of the original word?

2. Which of the highlighted words have prefixes?

Excerpt from *Red Pizzas for a Blue Count*
(Originally published in Italy by Edizioni Piemme *Una granita di mosche per il Conte*)

© 2015 Scholastic Education International (S) Pte Ltd ISBN 978-981-4629-67-6

are looking for a butler, a footman, and a maid."

"Great idea, little mouse!" I cried. "I will be the butler, you will be the footman, and Thea will be the maid."

 Look for the words in the word-search box using the clues given. Spaces are given to help you keep track.

X	G	D	H	Y	Z	A	W	U	W	P	X	Y
Q	Z	I	P	R	Y	T	R	N	M	N	U	R
M	I	S	U	N	D	E	R	S	T	A	N	D
G	W	S	W	X	K	S	D	E	U	S	C	F
K	P	A	Q	G	P	F	Z	E	N	P	O	U
J	M	T	V	L	J	Y	K	N	U	G	N	N
U	N	I	C	Y	C	L	E	W	S	C	V	I
S	H	S	G	D	H	N	V	C	U	B	I	C
Z	I	F	C	B	O	Q	A	P	A	K	N	O
U	N	I	F	O	R	M	D	Z	L	X	C	R
M	Q	E	B	L	S	P	W	E	H	J	E	N
N	F	D	Z	Q	F	R	E	M	I	N	D	D

1. There are nine words to look for. Three of the words start with the prefix "un-".

   _____   _____   _____

2. Look for these three words but remember to include their prefixes: understand, mind, satisfied.

   _____   _____   _____

3. Three of the words have a prefix that means "one".

   _____   _____   _____

A. The prefixes "mis-", "un-" and "dis-" usually mean "not". Which one would you place in front of the following words?

1. _____instructed   6. _____understand

2. _____seen   7. _____convinced

3. _____continue   8. _____professional

4. _____satisfied   9. _____checked

5. _____informed   10. _____usual

B. Some words can be combined with more than one prefix. However, the prefix used will change the meaning of the word. From the meanings given, fill in the blanks with the correct words.

1. (a) caused someone to believe in something again _____

    (b) not certain that something is true _____

2. (a) something that is raw _____

    (b) made a food dish again _____

3. (a) to vanish _____

    (b) to become visible once more _____

4. (a) instructed badly or incorrectly _____

    (b) someone who has not been taught _____

5. (a) not satisfied _____

    (b) unhappy with something _____

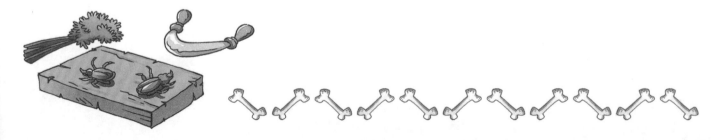

 Excerpt from *Red Pizzas for a Blue Count*
(Originally published in Italy by Edizioni Piemme *Una granita di mosche per il Conte*)

© 2015 Scholastic Education International (S) Pte Ltd ISBN 978-981-4629-67-6

A. **Fill in each blank with an appropriate word. Each one begins with the prefix "re-", which is affixed to a word that has been highlighted in the passage.**

1. After exiting through the sewers, Geronimo, Thea and Benjamin

   wanted to _____ their search for Trap.

2. Countess Snobella had already left the room but the hunchback

   _____ her to the room to speak with

   the visitors.

3. The hunchback had been fired before but no one else would work

   for the Ratoffs so they _____ him.

4. The young countess had already looked at their teeth but she

   decided to _____ at them.

B. **The prefix "uni-" means "one", "bi-" means "two", "tri-" means "three" and "poly-" means "many". Keeping this in mind, what do you think the following words mean?**

1. tri-colored

   _____

2. biannual

   _____

3. polygon

   _____

4. biennial

   _____

5. triangle

   _____

6. unicycle

   _____

© 2015 Scholastic Education International (S) Pte Ltd ISBN 978-981-4629-67-6

CROSSWORD TIME!

Complete the crossword.

Across

1. A person who has not been taught a subject is _____
2. Opposite of "sit down"
5. When Geronimo knocked, someone _____ _____ the door.
8. The hunchback _____ _____ the shadows.
12. Another way to say "to solve a problem" is "to _____ _____" a solution
15. To drink noisily
16. A loud metallic echoing sound
17. The sound a mouse makes

Down

1. Not up to the standards expected in a certain profession
3. Unnoticed
4. Benjamin _____ _____ down the corridor.
6. Chewed noisily on a piece of food
7. "Can you tell me how to _____ _____ the castle?" asked Thea.
9. To remember; to bring a memory back again
10. "Please _____ us _____ Castle Ratoff," said Benjamin.
11. "To _____ _____ straws" is to try any method to solve a problem, even if one knows it will not work.
13. They _____ down the blood greedily.
14. A large metallic disc that makes a deep booming sound when struck with a padded hammer

Excerpt from *Red Pizzas for a Blue Count*
(Originally published in Italy by Edizioni Piemme *Una granita di mosche per il Conte*)

Excerpt from *Red Pizzas for a Blue Count*
(Originally published in Italy by Edizioni Piemme *Una granita di mosche per il Conte*)

After making a big blunder with the city's Yellow Pages, I thought it best that I get out of town for a while. Trap, Thea, Benjamin, and I went in search of Claw Islands...

Next morning at dawn, I met everyone on the beach. Trap was bent over a pump trying to blow up a **huge balloon**. It was **purple** with **yellow dots**.

"What on earth is this? Where did you find it?" I shrieked.

"It's a hot-air balloon. I got it real cheap at the flea market," my cousin replied cheerfully.

I rolled my eyes. "I don't see why we have to travel in a hot-air balloon. And why did you pick such a horrible color? It looks like a giant prune with freckles!" To be honest, I was a little worried. It didn't seem like the safest way to travel. But Thea was already busy fixing a hole in the basket.

Benjamin posed in front of the balloon. "Uncle, would you take my picture?" he asked, grinning from ear to ear.

Half an hour later, we took off in the **balloon**. I sat the bottom of the basket and began writing in my diary. *6:25 A.M., we have just left the beach at New Mouse City. We are headed west for the Claw Islands.*

Day after day, I wrote down everything that happened in my journal. I figured writing would take my mind off traveling. Did I mention how much I hate to travel?

One way to learn new words is to think about the different **word forms** (noun, verb, adjective, adverb). Look at the verb "shriek". The noun form is also "shriek". When you change it to an adjective and an adverb, it is "shrieking" and "shriekingly" respectively.

Chew on it!

1. Both "peelable" and "peeling" are adjectives of the word "peel" but need to be used differently. What are the differences?

 Excerpt from *Attack of the Bandit Cats*
(Originally published in Italy by Edizioni Piemme *Il galeone dei gatti pirati*)

© 2015 Scholastic Education International (S) Pte Ltd ISBN 978-981-4629-67-6

Finally, at noon on the eleventh day, we caught sight of the Claw Islands. Trap jumped up and down as if he had just won the Mouse Lotto.

"The silver island should be somewhere around here! Keep your eyes peeled!" he shouted. "You, too, Gerry Berry. Although with your eyes you'd probably have trouble seeing Santa Mouse on his sleigh!" …

But then something totally strange happened. Zing! A cannonball flew by just above my ears!

Zinnnng! Zinnng! Two more cannonballs brushed by our balloon.

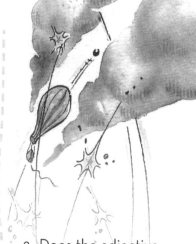

2. Does the adjective "brushlike" have a similar meaning to the "brush" used in the passage? Why?

Complete the table with the correct form of the words.

	Noun	Verb	Adjective
1		roll	
2			clean
3	writing		
4	market		
5		see	
6		take	
7			jumping
8			flying
9		excite	
10	reply		
11			traveling
12	fix		

Excerpt from *Attack of the Bandit Cats*
(Originally published in Italy by Edizioni Piemme *Il galeone dei gatti pirati*)

A. Which of the following words have an adverb form? Write the adverb in the blank. Insert an "X" for those that do not have one.

1. excite _____   6. cry _____

2. feeling _____   7. win _____

3. fix _____   8. worry _____

4. pump _____   9. pick _____

5. grin _____   10. clean _____

B. Fill in the blanks with the correct form – noun, verb, adjective or adverb – of the words in the brackets.

1. Thea gave her brother a _____ (winning) smile.

2. Geronimo ignored the _____ (shout) crowd and walked into his office.

3. The Black Bandit threw the apple into the air and swished his sword. The blade sliced _____ (clean) through the fruit.

4. Geronimo stayed at the bottom of the basket and kept _____ (write) in his journal throughout the _____ (fly).

5. Trap _____ (jump) up and down _____ (excite) when he thought they had found Claw Islands.

6. Benjamin _____ (roll) on the ground to catch up with the _____ (roll) stone that started on a _____ (roll) when it was kicked.

Excerpt from Attack of the Bandit Cats
(Originally published in Italy by Edizioni Piemme Il galeone dei gatti pirati)

© 2015 Scholastic Education International (S) Pte Ltd ISBN 978-981-4629-67-6

Is the word form correct in each of the following sentences? If it is not, write the correct form in the corresponding blank. Put a tick in the blank if the form is correct.

1. The <u>picked</u> apples sat on the table where the cats were stuffing their faces with snails.

   _____

2. Geronimo concentrated on his <u>written</u> so that he would not feel sick while in the hot-air balloon.

   _____

3. They <u>pumping</u> air into the balloon to get it into the air.

   _____

4. Geronimo always carried a notebook with him when he <u>traveling</u>.

   _____

5. Trap went to the place where all the <u>marketing</u> goods were being sold.

   _____

6. To pass the time in the balloon, Thea sang some songs <u>feeling</u>.

   _____

7. The island was just beyond their <u>seen</u>.

   _____

8. Benjamin was <u>excitable</u> about going on an adventure with his family.

   _____

9. As usual, Geronimo <u>worry</u> about everything.

   _____

10. After Thea <u>fixed</u> the hole in the balloon, they were ready to take off.

   _____

© 2015 Scholastic Education International (S) Pte Ltd ISBN 978-981-4629-67-6

Three Cheers for the Black Bandit!

Claw Island turned out to be a pirate ship … run by CATS! And now we were caught by them…

The nasty cat who had captured us was pushing us down a hallway. He stopped now and then to prick our tails with the point of his sword.

"Forward, you rodents!" he commanded. "You must pay your respects to His Excellency, Prince of All Pirates, Grand Duke of Deadly Deeds, Earl of Evil Matters, and let's not forget Baron of Broken Bones … the one and only Black Bandit!" He meowed solemnly.

My cousin put his paws on his hips. "So this prince character is your boss?" he scoffed. "Sounds like he needs to pick one name and stick with it! For your information, my name is **TRAP:**

T as in TAKE THAT, YOU CRAZY CAT!

R as in RUN FOR YOUR LIFE!

A as in ATTENTION, EVERYONE: HERE I COME!

P as in PAWS OFF IF YOU WANT TO LIVE!

The car sneered. "The Black Bandit will soon wipe that grin off your snout," he told my cousin. Trap just yawned and looked bored. He was a braver mouse than I. I was quaking in my Mouse Jordans!

Meanwhile, we had reached an enormous dining room. More than one hundred cats were stuffing their furry faces with food. At the head of the table sat a black cat. His fur was as black as a mouse hole at night. His long whiskers were dusted with golden

Idioms are expressions that have figurative meanings. Many are found in everyday speech e.g. "speak your mind" which means to say what you really think or feel. Idioms help to make language more colorful.

 Chew on it!

1. Do you think "paws on his hips" is an idiom? Why?

 Excerpt from *Attack of the Bandit Cats* (Originally published in Italy by Edizioni Piemme *Il galeone dei gatti pirati*)

 ISBN 978-981-4629-67-6

powder. He wore a cape of **black** silk and a large black hat with a golden feather on top. His shiny boots were decorated with buckles that JiNgLed at his every step. In short, he was the most terrifying creature I'd ever laid eyes on. But it got worse. Under his belt he carried a razor-sharp sword. And even scarier than *that* was the cat's right paw. It was a horrifying silver hook! ...

The Black Bandit stared straight into my eyes. One of his eyes was yellow and the other was green. It gave me the creeps.

2. Can you think of an idiom with the word "scare" in it?

 Each of the idioms contains an incorrect word. Circle the wrong word and replace it with the correct one. Then find the correct word in the word-search box.

W	E	X	M	I	N	D	G	X	C
Q	J	B	C	S	S	T	C	M	A
Z	X	O	X	I	I	S	A	G	T
F	C	A	U	Y	T	D	O	K	Q
I	E	T	E	A	R	P	K	B	F
N	E	P	B	K	U	B	C	R	B
G	G	K	Y	P	D	I	D	N	L
E	H	B	N	U	L	B	C	X	U
R	D	O	G	S	J	H	G	V	E
S	P	J	H	E	A	R	T	Z	K
C	N	R	I	P	F	Z	H	Y	B
J	Q	H	O	T	W	E	Y	E	A
B	F	K	R	C	A	K	E	Q	G
E	A	R	S	N	W	S	N	K	P
C	J	Q	F	T	O	N	G	U	E

1. curiosity killed the dog _____

2. slipped my foot _____

3. be in the same car _____

4. out of the orange _____

5. play by teeth _____

6. cat got your eyeball _____

7. be in cold water _____

8. a piece of brownie _____

9. cross your eyes _____

10. have a change of toes _____

11. be all fingers _____

12. see ear to ear _____

13. let the cat out of the cup _____

14. raining cats and sheep _____

Three Cheers for the Black Bandit!

A. **What do the following idioms mean? Match the correct meaning to each idiom by writing the correct letter in the blank.**

Idiom

1.	a piece of cake	_____	5.	wipe that grin off your face	_____
2.	pay your respects	_____	6.	play by ear	_____
3.	raining cats and dogs	_____	7.	see eye to eye	_____
4.	lay eyes on	_____	8.	cross your fingers	_____

Meaning

(a) see

(b) improvise or act accordingly

(c) make a polite visit to someone

(d) raining very heavily

(e) agree

(f) very easy

(g) stop smiling

(h) a gesture for good luck

B. **Fill in each blank with a suitable idiom from the box.**

let the cat out of the bag	I'm all ears	stuffing their faces
had a change of heart	in hot water	out of the blue

1. Geronimo and his family were _____ — they were being captured by cats!

2. The pirate cats were sitting at a long table, _____ with different snail dishes.

3. "_____," said the Black Bandit. "Tell me about your island."

4. Geronimo would not _____; he had to keep New Mouse City's location a secret.

5. A cannonball came flying at them _____.

6. The Black Bandit looked like he was going to eat the mice but then he _____.

 Excerpt from *Attack of the Bandit Cats*
(Originally published in Italy by Edizioni Piemme *Il galeone dei gatti pirati*) ISBN 978-981-4629-67-6

For each question, create one sentence that contains two of the idioms indicated. Be sure to use the correct forms of the words.

1.   play by ear / be in the same boat

    _____

    _____

2.   give me the creeps / curiosity killed the cat

    _____

    _____

3.   quaking in my boots / be in hot water

    _____

    _____

4.   be all ears / slipped my mind

    _____

    _____

5.   stuff my face / have a change of heart

    _____

    _____

© 2015 Scholastic Education International (S) Pte Ltd ISBN 978-981-4629-67-6

Excerpt from *Attack of the Bandit Cats*
(Originally published in Italy by Edizioni Piemme *Il galeone dei gatti pirati*)

We had been captured by the cats. Would we survive being in the midst of our mortal enemies?

It was Prowls, the **Black Bandit's** brother.

"Mice at last! No more snails!" he meowed.

"*Keep quiet, you nitwit!*" snapped the **Bandit**. Then he turned to us.

"Four **plump** mice," he murmured. He looked down at his sharp claws as if he were longing for a nail file. Then he glanced at a cat in an apron who was huffing and puffing in the corner. He was busy roasting a long rod of snails over a fire.

"So tell me, where are you from?" asked the **Bandit**, curling his tail into a question mark.

Just then, Prowls began dancing around the room in a swirl of yellow. He stopped in front of Trap and pricked him with his sword. "What's wrong? Cat got your tongue?"

I glanced at my cousin. He was snorting like Scar Rat, the famous boxer, before a big match. "If you were on our island, you wouldn't have a tongue!" Trap shrieked.

"Jumping tuna fish!" cried the **Black Bandit**. "Do you mean you are from Mouse Island? Our ship has been searching for ages for that place! It sounds amazing!" … "So, tell us where your island is. We will take you back immediately," he purred.

Adverbs give more information about actions or things. For example, "very" is added to "contagious" to show how fast the disease had spread.

Adverbs of place tell where an action is taking place.

 Chew on it!

1. Which adverbs could you add to "pricked" that would give more information about the manner in which Prowls did this action?

 Excerpt from *Attack of the Bandit Cats*
(Originally published in Italy by Edizioni Piemme *Il galeone dei gatti pirati*)

© 2015 Scholastic Education International (S) Pte Ltd ISBN 978-981-4629-67-6

"Oh, we don't want to go back," I said, pretending not to care.

"And why not?" asked the **Bandit**, narrowing his eyes.

"Well, you see, the four of us are the only survivors of a terrible sickness," I whispered, thinking quickly. We had to stop these bandit cats from finding Mouse Island! "Yes, **acutis fungus mousitis**, a very contagious disease, has wiped out the whole population. So we left, hoping to find another island of rodents." I wiped away a fake tear. …

"So there are no more mice on the island?" he mumbled, **DRUMMING** the table with his claws.

2. "The disease was _____." What one-word adverb of place can show how widespread the disease was?

Fill in the missing letters then find the words in the word-search box.

I	Q	A	C	S	A	Y	H	J	B	U
N	B	N	H	L	L	O	U	D	L	Y
S	D	O	P	O	J	K	R	P	Q	W
I	K	W	S	W	V	C	R	C	U	P
D	G	H	E	L	A	X	I	S	I	O
E	V	E	R	Y	W	H	E	R	E	U
Z	J	R	I	A	C	G	D	Y	T	T
L	B	E	O	B	D	R	L	C	L	S
A	H	V	U	C	K	T	Y	T	Y	I
T	U	P	S	T	A	I	R	S	A	D
E	N	A	L	B	K	D	B	G	J	E
L	C	J	Y	S	X	G	V	R	B	Z
Y	D	O	W	N	S	T	A	I	R	S

1. l _ t e _ y
2. q _ _ _ t l _
3. _ v _ r y w _ e r _
4. _ u r r _ _ _ l y
5. u _ s _ _ i r s
6. _ o _ h _ r e
7. s _ _ i o u s _ _
8. i n _ _ _ _ _
9. _ _ w n s t _ _ r _
10. _ _ o w _ y
11. _ o u _ l y
12. _ _ t s _ d _

Excerpt from *Attack of the Bandit Cats*
(Originally published in Italy by Edizioni Piemme *Il galeone dei gatti pirati*)

A. **Fill in each blank with an adverb from the box. You need not use all of them.**

loudly	lately	immediately	seriously	very
only	quietly	quickly	hurriedly	slowly

1. The four mice were the _____ survivors of the devastating disease.

2. The cats were munching _____ and making such a noise that it was deafening.

3. Prowls was jumping around so _____ that he looked like a blur of yellow.

4. When the mice were captured, they were brought _____ to the Black Bandit.

5. Geronimo answered the Black Bandit's question so _____ that the cat could not tell if the mouse was joking.

6. Chef Slobbertooth moved _____ from the kitchen when he was summoned by his captain because Black Bandit didn't like to wait.

B. **Fill in each blank with an adverb of place.**

Our captor took us 1. _____ below the deck. We were brought

2. _____ the enormous dining room.

There were cats 3. _____! We were very

scared, and the Black Bandit terrified us even more. When

we stood 4. _____ _____ _____ him,

he questioned us till we had nothing left to say. "Take them

back 5. _____ and to the jail cells."

he hollered. As we turned to leave, I looked around for Trap

but he was 6. _____ to be seen.

Excerpt from *Attack of the Bandit Cats*
(Originally published in Italy by Edizioni Piemme *Il galeone dei gatti pirati*)

© 2015 Scholastic Education International (S) Pte Ltd ISBN 978-981-4629-67-6

Form sentences that contain all the adverbs stated for each question.

1. slowly / in front of

    _____

    _____

2. immediately / upstairs

    _____

    _____

3. lately / everywhere

    _____

    _____

4. very / quietly / over

    _____

    _____

5. loudly / outside

    _____

    _____

6. quickly / nowhere

    _____

    _____

© 2015 Scholastic Education International (S) Pte Ltd ISBN 978-981-4629-67-6

Excerpt from *Attack of the Bandit Cats*
(Originally published in Italy by Edizioni Piemme *Il galeone dei gatti pirati*)

Find the Treasure

While exploring, Benjamin found a piece of paper with some cryptic clues and a map with symbols for each place on the ship. However, a number of the words and phrases had been smeared. Can you help Benjamin figure out what these are? Fill in each blank with an appropriate word from the box.

quickly	slowly	fixedly	inside	in	write
eye to eye	roll	grinning	over	on	in front of
jump	pick	feel	only	cross your fingers	

There is treasure 1. _____ one of the cabins.

Start 2. _____ the kitchen. 3.

_____ up and down on the red tile under

the onion basket. Take 4. _____ the gold marker

from the drawer that opens. Do not take the other colored markers.

Go to the first room across from the kitchen. Stand 5. _____ the mirror

and 6. _____. Using the marker, 7. _____ "BB"

8. _____ the wall where the shadow of your crossed fingers appears.

Enter Whiskers's Lounge and Pool Room (it has a symbol with a 9. _____

cat's head placed 10. _____ waves). Stare 11. _____

at the cat's head. Make sure you position your head at the same level so you can look

12. _____ with the cat. A pin will drop out of its mouth.

Next, enter the Captain's quarters. Use the pin to 13. _____

the lock of the spider's cage. 14. _____ around

the bottom of the cage and press the button.

Excerpt from *Attack of the Bandit Cats*
(Originally published in Italy by Edizioni Piemme *Il galeone dei gatti pirati*)

A heavy gold cannon will

15._____ out

16._____. Take the cannon

and enter the room directly across.

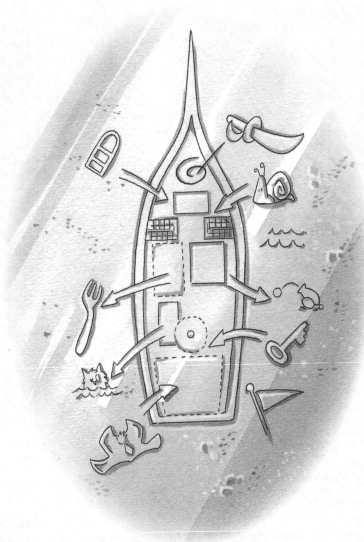

A secret compartment has been revealed! Place the cannon in the bowl. Into the microphone, say the idioms that mean "raining very heavily" and "let the secret out". On the screen, draw the symbol for this room. Part of the wall will move. You've found the treasure!

17.   What was the symbol that you had to draw on the screen? _____

18.   What were the two idioms that you had to say into the microphone?

_____

_____

Answers

Section 1

Unit 1

Pages 6–7

Chew on it! questions:

1. The camp was a very dirty and smelly place.
2. *Accept all reasonable answers.* He felt that nobody in their right mind would want to go for a horrible course like that.

A 1. Exhausted 2. Overhanging 3. Underground
4. Panic-stricken 5. Jungle 6. Leafy
7. Terrified 8. Venomous 9. Moldy 10. Rotting

B.

```
        B
O V E R H A N G I N G
        A
        T
        E       R
V E N O M O U S
        T       M O L D Y
        T       E
        I       L
        N       L
        G       Y
```

Page 8

A. 1. exhausted 2. leafy 3. rare 4. muddy 5. terrified

B. Accept all reasonable answers.
   1. rotting 2. cement 3. anxious 4. poisonous 5. buried

Page 9

The following are suggested answers.

1. To help Geronimo overcome his fear of everything, Thea, Trap and Benjamin <u>sent him on this crazy survival course in the jungle.</u>
2. When Geronimo was told he had to attend the survival camp, <u>he was terrified.</u>
3. Penelope was clearly crazy! Her idea of <u>a wake-up call was an icy bucketful of water in the face!</u>
4. Instead of <u>getting them to walk on a paved road</u>, Penelope made the recruits run on the muddy track.
5. It was so hot that Geornimo longed to <u>look for shade under the leafy trees.</u>
6. The trees with their <u>overhanging branches made the jungle look scary and dark.</u>

Unit 2

Pages 10–11

Chew on it! questions:

1. hold 2. acceptable, exceptional, great

Word cline:
- squeaked → told → demanded
- wailed → sobbed → cried → whimpered
- smiled → grinned → beamed

Page 12

1. smiled, grinned, beamed 2. grinned, smiled 3. beamed
4. trunk, branches, twigs 5. twigs, branches 6. trunk
7. starving 8. famished, hungry 9. peckish

Page 13

1. sob (3); cry (2); wail (4); whimper (1)
2. mishap (2); disaster (3); misfortune (1)
3. tell (2); demand (3); squeak (1)

Unit 3

Pages 14–15

Chew on it! questions:

1. trees, rocks 2. lips, mouth, chin and so on

A.

```
        S N A K E S
      R O D E N T S
        B I R D S
        M O N K E Y S
        R A T S
C R O C O D I L E S
      T I G E R S
```

B.

fur · whiskers · paw · snout · tail

C. (Clockwise from top) North, Northeast, East, Southeast, South, Southwest, West, Northwest

Page 16

A. 1. bird 2. mouse 3. fish 4. mouse 5. bird
6. fish 7. deer 8. bird 9. fish 10. deer

B. 1. Trees 2. forest 3. Monkeys
4. snakes 5. birds 6. rodent

Page 17

1. East, West 2. Southwest
3. Southeast, South 4. Northwest, Northeast

Activity 1

Pages 18–19

A. 1. muddy 2. overhanging 3. cried 4. underground
5. snouth, paved 6. sobbing, tail 7. wailed, disaster

B. 1. crazy 2. army 3. terrified 4. jungle
5. venomous 6. spiders 7. scorpions 8. crocodiles
9. monkeys 10. North 11. South 12. East 13. West 14. very tall 15. branches

Section 2

Unit 4

Pages 20–21

Chew on it! questions:

1. I thought we were better friends than that.
2. thinnest, most famous

```
P U M O F U R R I E R M O
O L A U R D E R A C S E R
P A F S E W O R S E N E A
E R E B I T E R O M R E T
R M R I L A L E N T E D   END
O A O G L L B A V E I I R
M D M G I E↓N B E L U E
R D R E S M M U E R O I I
E E R R O O T E R M C K
T R I F E R R S A F Y I C
T S R U I E B A D L E A
E C A N N B H E R O M R W
B G N I R O A N D S O M E
```

Page 22

A. 1. most famous 2. worst 3. juiciest
4. most badly 5. best

B. 1. madder 2. most boring 3. most scared
4. silliest 5. scarier 6. more talented

Page 23

1. *The Rodent's Gazette* is more popular than *The Daily Rat.*
   The Rodent's Gazette is the most popular newspaper in New Mouse City.
2. Thea told a wackier story than Trap.
   Thea told the wackiest story of them all.
3. Trap is funnier than Geronimo.
   Trap is the funniest in the family.
4. Benjamin is a faster runner than Thea.
   Benjamin is the fastest runner in his class.
5. Geronimo's story is more unbelievable than Benjamin's.
   Geronimo's story is the most unbelievable of all stories.

Unit 5

Page 24

Chew on it! questions:

1. continue 2. answered

© 2015 Scholastic Education International (S) Pte Ltd ISBN 978-981-4629-67-6

Page 25

1. BROADSHEET   2. REFUSE BIN   3. INCOMPETENT
4. TRUSTWORTHY   5. TABLOID   6. EXCLAIMED
7. SNORTED   8. TRASH CAN   9. GRUNTED
10. RESPECTABLE 11. UNEDUCATED   12. GASPED

The two synonyms are: respectable and trustworthy

Page 26

1. broadsheet   2. newspaper   3. paper   4. tabloid
5. trustworthy 6. reputable   7. honorable 8. respectable
9. incompetent 10. uneducated 11. ignorant 12. illiterate

Page 27

A. 1. indecent   2. intelligent   3. literate   4. educated

B. 1. untrustworthy   2. dishonorable   3. disreputable
   4. competent   5. intelligent

C. 1. garbage bin   2. popular
   3. challenged   4. horrible

Unit 6
Pages 28–29

Chew on it! questions:
1. clothes do not make a man
2. Yes, because it is ironic that crumbs should be considered something to treasure.

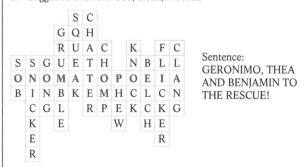

Page 30

A. 1. having a good time
   2. fifty dollars
   3. you cannot judge a person by his appearance
   4. to do something honestly and sincerely
   5. to make payment for a purchase

B. 1. knitted my brows
   2. down in the dumps; collapsed into a heap
   3. cost an arm and a leg
   4. over the moon; the apple of his eye
   5. high and mighty; not up to scratch

Page 31

A. 1. happy   2. favorite   3. miserable
   4. frowned   5. respectable

B. Accept all reasonable answers.

Activity 2
Pages 32–33

wackiest <u>7</u>   most talented <u>4</u>   not up to scratch <u>6</u>
wackier <u>5</u>   unbelievable <u>1</u>   wacky <u>2</u>
kicking up his paws <u>3</u>

Section 3
Unit 7
Pages 34–35

Chew on it! questions:
1. To look at or examine something
2. Popped in — to go in somewhere for a short while
   Popped out — to go out for a short while
   Popped over, popped round — to visit

(crossword grid)

```
      C H E C K
P U L L   L               K
A     I   U     L     F   E
S     M   T     O     I   E
S     B   C     O   G U L P
      S H A K E     U
  G E T       A     R
  I     A   D I R E C T
C A M E   D I S A P P E A R
            O         N
      S C A M P E R
```

Page 36

A. 1. rolled up   2. stood up   3. checked
   4. keep away   5. popped   6. climbed

B. 1. scamper off   2. gulped   3. turned out
   4. shake off   5. pull out   6. disappeared

Page 37

1. away   2. out   3. up   4. around   5. by
6. down   7. off   8. way   9. up   10. away
11. out   12. off   13. back   14. into   15. out
16. after 17. through 18. down 19. for   20. up

Unit 8
Pages 38–39

Chew on it! questions:
1. No. To bounce is an action rather than the sound of something bouncing.
2. *Suggested answers:* boo, creak, whoosh

Sentence:
GERONIMO, THEA AND BENJAMIN TO THE RESCUE!

Pages 40–41

A. 1. yummy   2. whisper   3. clang   4 sob   5. phew
   6. chomp   7. whoosh   8. slink   9. shriek   10. chatter

B. 1. flicker   2. grumbled   3. gong
   4. snicker   5. slunk   6. slurped

Accept all reasonable answers for triple-cheese activity.

Unit 9
Pages 42–43

Chew on it! questios:
1. "unthink" is to not think, while "rethink" is to think about something again.
2. unusual, reminds, disappeared

(word search grid)

```
X G D H Y Z A W U W P X Y
Q Z I P R Y T R N M N U R
M I S U N D E R S T A N D
G W S W X K S D E U S C F
K P A Q G P F Z E N P O U
J M T V L J Y K N U G N N
U N I C Y C L E W S C V I
S H S G D H N V C U B I C
Z I F C B O Q A P A K N O
U N I F O R M D Z L X C R
M Q E B L S P W E H J E N
N F D Z Q F R E M I N D D
```

1. unusual; unconvinced; unseen
2. misunderstand; remind; dissatisfied
3. unicorn; uniform; unicyle

63

Page 44

A.
1. misinstructed / uninstructed 2. unseen
3. discontinue 4. dissatisfied / unsatisfied
5. uninformed / misinformed 6. misunderstand
7. unconvinced 8. unprofessional
9. unchecked 10. unusual

B.
1a. reconvinced 1b. unconvinced
2a. uncooked 2b. recooked
3a. disappear 3b. reappear
4a. misinstructed 4b. uninstructed
5a. dissatisfied 5b. unsatisfied

Page 45

A.
1. recontinue 2. recalled 3. rehired 4. relook

B.
1. Having three colors 2. Twice yearly
3. A shape with many sides
4. Refers to an event that happens once every two years
   or lasts for two years
5. A shape with three angles
6. A type of vehicle with only one wheel

Activity 3
Pages 46–47

```
U N I N S T R U C T E D
N               S T A N D U P
P       S       N
R       C A M E T O       N
O       A               E       C
F       M   G           E       H
D I S A P P E A R E D I N T O
I   S   E   T   E   I           M
S   S   R   T   C   R           P
S   I   E   T   A   E           E
A   O   D   O   L   C           D
T   N   A   O   L   T
I   A   L   F   L   T   C   L
S       F I G U R E O U T   G
F       U           C   U   O
I     S L U R P       H   N
E       P       C L A N G
D   S Q U E A K       T
        D
```

Section 4
Unit 10
Pages 48–49

Chew on it! questions:
1. "Peelable" indicates that something can be peeled, but "peeling" as an adjective means that something is losimg its outer layer.
2. No. "Brushlike" means that something has the quality and likeness of a brush. In the passage however, the verb "brush" means to touch something quickly and lightly.

	Noun	Verb	Adjective
1	roll	roll	rolling
2	cleanliness	clean	clean
3	writing	write	written/writable
4	market	market	marketing
5	sight	see	seeing
6	take	take	taken/takeable
7	jump	jump	jumping
8	flight	fly	flying
9	excitement	excite	exciting/excited
10	reply	reply	replying
11	travel	travel	traveling
12	fix	fix	fixed

Page 50

A.
1. excitedly / excitingly 2. feelingly
3. fixedly 4. X 5. grinningly
6. cryingly 7. winningly 8. worryingly
9. X 10. cleanly

B.
1. winning 2. shouting 3. cleanly
4. writing, flight 5. jumped, excitedly 6. rolled, rolling, roll

Page 51

1. √ 2. writing 3. pumped 4. traveled 5. √
6. feelingly 7. sight 8. excited 9. worried 10. √

Unit 11
Pages 52-53

1. dog → cat
2. foot → mind
3. car → boat
4. orange → blue
5. teeth → ear
6. eyeball → tongue
7. cold → hot
8. brownie → cake
9. eyes → fingers
10. toes → heart
11. fingers → ears
12. ear → eye
13. cup → bag
14. sheep → dogs

```
W E X M I N D G X C
Q J B C S S T C M A
Z X O X I I S A G T
F C A U Y T D O K Q
I E T E A R P K B F
N E P B K U B C R B
G G K Y P D I D N L
E H B N U L B C X U
R D O G S J H G V E
S P J H E A R T Z K
C N R I P F Z H Y B
J Q H O T W E Y E A
B F K R C A K E Q G
E A R S N W S N K P
C J Q F T O N G U E
```

Page 54

A.
1. f 2. c 3. d 4. a 5. g 6. b 7. e 8. h

B.
1. in hot water 2. stuffing their faces
3. I'm all ears 4. let the cat out of the bag
5. out of the blue 6. had a change of heart

Page 55

Accept all reasonable answers.

Unit 12
Pages 56–57

Chew on it! questions:
1. Suggested answers: repeatedly, lightly 2. everywhere

```
I Q A C S A Y H J B U
N B N H L L O U D L Y
S D O P O J K R P Q W
I K W S W V C R C U P
D G H E L A X I S I O
E V E R Y W H E R E U
Z J R I A C G D Y T T
L B E O B D R L C L S
A H V U C K T Y T Y I
T U P S T A I R S A D
E N A L B K D B G J E
L C J Y S X G V R B Z
Y D O W N S T A I R S
```

1. lately
2. quietly
3. everywhere
4. hurriedly
5. upstairs
6. nowhere
7. seriously
8. inside
9. downstairs
10. slowly
11. loudly
12. outside

Page 58

A.
1. only 2. loudly 3. quickly
4. immediately 5. seriously 6. hurriedly

B.
1. downstairs 2. inside 3. everywhere
4. in front of 5. upstairs 6. nowhere

Page 59

Accept all reasonable answers.

Activity 4
Pages 60–61

1. inside 2. in 3. Jump 4. only
5. in front of 6. cross your fingers 7. write 8. on
9. grinning 10. over 11. fixedly 12. eye to eye
13. pick 14. Feel 15. roll 16. slowly
17. a fork 18. raining cats and dogs/let the cat out of the bag

© 2015 Scholastic Education International (S) Pte Ltd ISBN 978-981-4629-67-6

Glossary

Unit 1: I'm Afraid of Bugs! (Descriptive words)

army	referring to an organized military force
beaten	well-trodden or much used
crazy	mad or insane
exhausted	very tired
jungle	an area of land with dense forests
leafy	having many leaves
moldy	covered with a fungal growth that causes decay
muddy	covered in or full of mud
overhanging	extending outwards over
panic-stricken	very frightened, affected greatly with panic
paved	covered with flat stones or bricks
rare	not occurring very often
rotting	decaying
smelly	having an unpleasant smell
terrified	very scared
tired	in need of rest
underground	beneath the surface of the ground
venomous	poisonous
very tall	having extremely great height
wake-up	serving to rouse someone out of a reverie or sleep

Unit 2: Day 2: Tuesday (Word clines)

beam	to smile radiantly
branch	the part growing out of the trunk of a tree
cry	to shed tears, either from sorrow, distress or pain
demand	to say something to someone in an authoritative manner
disaster	an event that happens suddenly and causes great suffering and loss to many people
famished	extremely hungry
grin	to smile broadly
hungry	feeling a need for food
misfortune	an unfortunate event
mishap	an unlucky accident
peckish	a little hungry
smile	form one features into a pleasant or amused expression, usually with the corners of the mouth upturned
sob	to cry noisily with short gasps
squeak	to say something to someone in a high-pitched voice, usually from nervousness
starving	dying of hunger
tell	to say something to someone in a normal tone of voice
trunk	main stem of the tree
twig	small woody shoot growing from the branch of a tree
wail	to make a loud, long cry of sadness or pain
whimper	to make a quiet crying sound

Unit 3: Day 4: Thursday (Hyponyms)

bird	an animal usually characterized by its feathers, wings, and beak
crocodile	a large reptile with a long jaw and tail, short legs and horny textured skin
East	the direction to the right of North, and the direction the sun rises in
fur	the short fine hair found on an animal
monkey	a small- or medium-sized primate with a long tail
North	the direction the compass needle usually points to
Northeast	the direction lying between North and East
Northwest	the direction lying between North and West
paw	an animal's foot
rat	an animal from the rodent family that looks like a large mouse
rodent	a category of animals characterized by the constantly growing incisors and lack of canine teeth
snake	a long limbless reptile that slithers on the ground
snout	the projecting nose and mouth of an animal
South	the direction opposite of North
Southeast	the direction lying between South and East
Southwest	the direction lying between South and West
tail	the hindmost part of an animal, that is prolonged beyond the body
tiger	a very large feline that has yellow-brown fur with black stripes
West	the direction to the left of North, and the direction the sun sets in
whiskers	the long projecting bristles growing from the face or snout of an animal

Unit 4: Trouble at The Nibbler (Comparative and Superlative adjectives)

the words in brackets are the comparative and superlative forms respectively

bad	of poor quality or low standard (worse; worst)
badly	in an unsatisfactory or inadequate way (more badly; most badly)
big	of a considerable size (bigger; biggest)
boring	not interesting (more boring; most boring)
famous	known by many people (more famous; most famous)
fast	moving at a high speed (faster; fastest)
funny	causing laughter or amusement (funnier; funniest)
furry	covered with fur (furrier; furriest)
good	having the required qualities or of a high standard (better; best)
handsome	good-looking (more handsome; most handsome)
juicy	full of juice (juicier; juiciest)
mad	angry (madder; maddest)

© 2015 Scholastic Education International (S) Pte Ltd ISBN 978-981-4629-67-6

neat	tidy or in good order (neater; neatest)
popular	liked by many people (more popular; most popular)
scared	frightened (more scared; most scared)
scary	frightening (scarier; scariest)
silly	absurd and foolish (sillier; silliest)
talented	having a natural aptitude or skill for something (more talented; most talented)
unbelievable	not to be believed (more unbelievable; most unbelievable)
wacky	funny in an odd way (wackier; wackiest)

Unit 5: A Thick-headed Furbrain (Synonyms)

broadsheet	a regular printed publication made up of folded unstapled sheets that normally contains news, articles and advertisements
exclaim	cry out suddenly, either in surprise, pain or strong emotion
garbage can	a dustbin
gasp	catch one's breath, usually from pain or asthonishment
grunt	make a low, short guttural sound
honorable	having honesty and good moral character
ignorant	lacking information or knowledge
illiterate	lacking the ability to read or write
incompetent	lacking the necessary skills or ability to do something
newspaper	a regular printed publication that normally deals with serious subjects
paper	the shortened form of "newspaper"
refuse bin	a receptacle for waste matter
reputable	having a good reputation
respectable	having a decent character, appearance or behavior
snort	make an explosive sound through one's nose, especially to show indignation
tabloid	a regular printed publication that usually has sensational stories
thick-headed	unintelligent or stupid
trash can	a receptacle for rubbish
trustworthy	having a dependable nature
uneducated	lacking a high level of education

Unit 6: Stilton, Old Pal... (Figurative expressions)

apple of one's eye	favorite
close to one's heart	favorite or of deep interest to someone
clothes do not make the man	a person's appearance does not reflect who he or she really is
collapse into a heap	slump
cost an arm and a leg	expensive
down in the dumps	feeling miserable
fifty smackers	fifty dollars
furrow the brows	frown
give a talking to	scold

high and mighty	stuck-up
in good standing	respectable
in high spirits	happy
kicking up your heels	having a good time or doing something you enjoy
knit the brows	frown
moving pictures	movies
not up to scratch	awful; not of a good standard
of good repute	respectable
on good faith	with good intent
out of sorts	feeling miserable or unhappy
over the moon	happy or joyous
settle your bill	make payment
sewer rats	used to describe people who are dirty, useless and disgusting

Unit 7: Garlic, Garlic, and More Garlic (Phrasal verbs)

check out	to go to a place to see what it is like
climb down	to descend
clutch at	to grasp and hold tight
come to	to appear at
direct to	to point in the direction of
disappear into	to cease to be visible
figure out	to find the solution or discover
get to	to travel to
gulp down	to swallow in large mouthfuls
keep away	to make someone or something stay away
look at	to observe someone or something so as to form an opinion
look for	to seek or search for
pass by	to move past
pop out	to give the appearance of protruding out
pull out	to take out
roll up	to indicate the act of rolling, of something being accumulated
scamper off	to run with quick light steps in a particular direction
shake off	to get rid of
stand up	to rise to an upright position
turn out	to switch off

Unit 8: Gonnnggg! Gonnnggg! (Onomatopoiea)

belch	the sound of someone emitting wind noisily from the stomach
chatter	the sound of teeth clicking together repeatedly due to the cold
chomp	the sound of someone chewing very loudly
clang	a loud and rather prolonged metallic sound
flicker	to show something emitting light unsteadily
gong	a resounding noise emitted when a gong is struck
grumble	to indicate that someone is complaining unhappily
gulp	the sound made when one swallows air quickly

© 2015 Scholastic Education International (S) Pte Ltd   ISBN 978-981-4629-67-6

knock	the sound of someone striking a surface so as to attract attention
phew	the sound to indicate that someone is relieved
shiver	to show someone shaking from the cold
shriek	a high-pitched sound uttered in fear
slink	the sound to indicate a smooth, gliding movement
slurp	a sucking sound made when drinking
snicker	a quiet and disrespectful laugh
sob	the sound of one crying noisily to the point of gasping
squeak	a short, shrill cry like that of a mouse
whisper	the sound of someone speaking softly, using his or her breath
whoosh	the sound made by something that is moving quickly
yummy	a sound to indicate that something is delicious

Unit 9: Please, Let Me Faint in Peace! (Prefixes)

disappear	to vanish
discontinue	to stop making or offering something; to end
dissatisfied	unhappy with something
misintruct	instruct badly or incorrectly
misunderstand	fail to understand correctly
re-entrance	the act of entering a place again
re-hire	to employ again
re-knock	to strike on a surface again so as to attract attention
reappear	to become visible once more
recall	to remember something from the past
recheck	to examine again
reconvince	to cause someone to believe in something again
recook	made a dish again
relook	to direct one's eyes in a particular direction once more
remind	to make someone remember something again
unchecked	something that is not restrained
unconvinced	not certain that something is true
uncooked	something that is raw
unicorn	a mythical animal that looks like a horse, with a single horn protruding from its head
unicycle	a single-wheeled cycle
uniform	to have the same form
uninstructed	someone who has not been taught
unprofessional	below or against the standards expected for a particular profession
unsatisfied	not satisfied
unseen	not seen or noticed
unusual	not usual or normal

Unit 10: We Leave at Dawn (Word forms)

n = noun; v = verb; adj = adjective; adv = adverb

clean (v)	to free from marks or dirt [cleanliness (n); clean (adj); cleanly (adv)]
cry (v)	to call out loudly [cry (n); crying (adj); cryingly (adv)]
excitement (n)	the state of feeling eager enthusiasm [excite (v); excited/exciting (adj); excitedly/excitingly (adv)]
feeling (n)	an emotional state or reaction [feeling (v); feeling (adj); feelingly (adv)]
fix (v)	to mend [fix (n); fixed (adj); fixedly (adv)]
fly (v)	to move through the air [flight (n); flying (adj)]
grin (v)	to smile broadly [grin (n); grinning (adj); grinningly (adv)]
happen (v)	occur or take place [happening (n); happening (adj)]
jump (v)	to spring into the air [jump (n); jumping (adj)]
market (n)	a place where products are bought and sold [market (v); market/marketing (adj)]
pick (v)	to choose [pick (n); picked (adj)]
pump (n)	a mechanical device used to inject air into balloons [pump (v); pumping (adj)]
reply (v)	to answer [reply (n); replying (adj)]
roll (v)	to move your eyes upwards so as to show disbelief or annoyance [roll (n); rolling (adj)]
shout (v)	to say something loudly [shout (n); shouting (adj)]
sight (n)	glimpse or view [see (v); seeing (adj)]
take (v)	occupy or make less [take (n); taken/takeable (adj)]
travel (v)	make a journey [travel (n); traveling (adj)]
win (v)	to get the top prize [win (n); winning (adj); winningly (adv)]
worry (v)	to feel anxiety [worry (n); worrying (adj); worryingly (adv)]
write (v)	to make marks that represent letters, numbers or words on a surface [writing (n); written/writable (adj)]

Unit 11: Three Cheers for the Black Bandit! (Idioms)

a piece of cake	very easy
be in hot water	be in trouble
be in the same boat	to be in the same, usually unpleasant, situation as someone else
cat got your tongue	a comment made when someone is unusually quiet
cross your fingers	a gesture for good luck
curiosity killed the cat	to indicate that being curious about something can get you into trouble
give you the creeps	to make someone feel frightened or anxious
have a change of heart	to change your attitude toward or decision about something

lay eyes on	to see
let the cat out of the bag	to reveal a secret by accident
out of the blue	all of a sudden
pay your respects	to make a polite visit to someone
play by ear	improvise or act accordingly
quake in your boots	to be very frightened or anxious
raining cats and dogs	raining very heavily
run for your life	to run away to save your life
see eye to eye	agree
slip your mind	to forget
stuff your faces	to overeat or eat greedily
to be all ears	to listen carefully and eagerly
wipe that grin off your face	stop smiling

Unit 12: No More Snails! (Adverbs)

downstairs	to indicate the lower floor of a structure
everywhere	all places
hurriedly	in a hasty manner
immediately	at once or instantly
in	to indicate one thing being enclosed or surrounded by something else
in front of	in a position just ahead of something
inside	interior or the inner part of something
lately	not long ago
loudly	in a manner that makes a lot of noise
nowhere	not in any place
on	to indicate one thing is located on the surface of something else
only	solely; no one or nothing more
outside	exterior or the outer part of something
over	to indicate one thing is above something else
quicky	at a fast pace
quietly	in a manner that makes little or no noise
seriously	in a solemn manner
slowly	at a slow pace
upstairs	to indicate the upper floor of a structure
very	used to indicate emphasis

© 2015 Scholastic Education International (S) Pte Ltd ISBN 978-981-4629-67-6